LET'S QUILT!

Easy Projects
for First-Time Quilters

ANN KISRO

Martingale®
& COMPANY

Let's Quilt! Easy Projects for First-Time Quilters
© 2006 by Ann Kisro

Martingale®
& COMPANY

That Patchwork Place

That Patchwork Place® is an imprint of
Martingale & Company®.

Martingale & Company
20205 144th Avenue NE
Woodinville, WA 98072-8478 USA
www.martingale-pub.com

Printed in China
11 10 09 08 07 06   8 7 6 5 4 3 2 1

Library of Congress Cataloging-in-Publication Data
Kisro, Ann.
  Let's quilt : easy projects for first-time quilters / Ann Kisro.
     p. cm.
  ISBN 1-56477-651-4
1. Patchwork—Patterns. 2. Quilting—Patterns. I. Title.
  TT835.K535 2006
  746.46—dc22
                          2005028417

Mission Statement

Dedicated to providing quality products and service to inspire creativity.

Credits

President	Nancy J. Martin
CEO	Daniel J. Martin
VP and General Manager	Tom Wierzbicki
Publisher	Jane Hamada
Editorial Director	Mary V. Green
Managing Editor	Tina Cook
Technical Editor	Laurie Baker
Copy Editor	Melissa Bryan
Design Director	Stan Green
Illustrator	Laurel Strand
Cover and Text Designer	Trina Craig
Photographer	Brent Kane

Acknowledgments

A big thank-you to:

Mom and Dad, Susan and Jim Kisro, for everything.

Mom, for your long-arm machine quilting and for helping with samples.

Shirley Snyder, for making a sample quilt and for your continuing encouragement.

Madeline Dostal, for letting me borrow your quilt for this book.

Martingale & Company, for giving me this opportunity and to everyone there who worked hard to create this book.

D. Holmes Meir Photography (www.dholmesmeir.com), for the author photo.

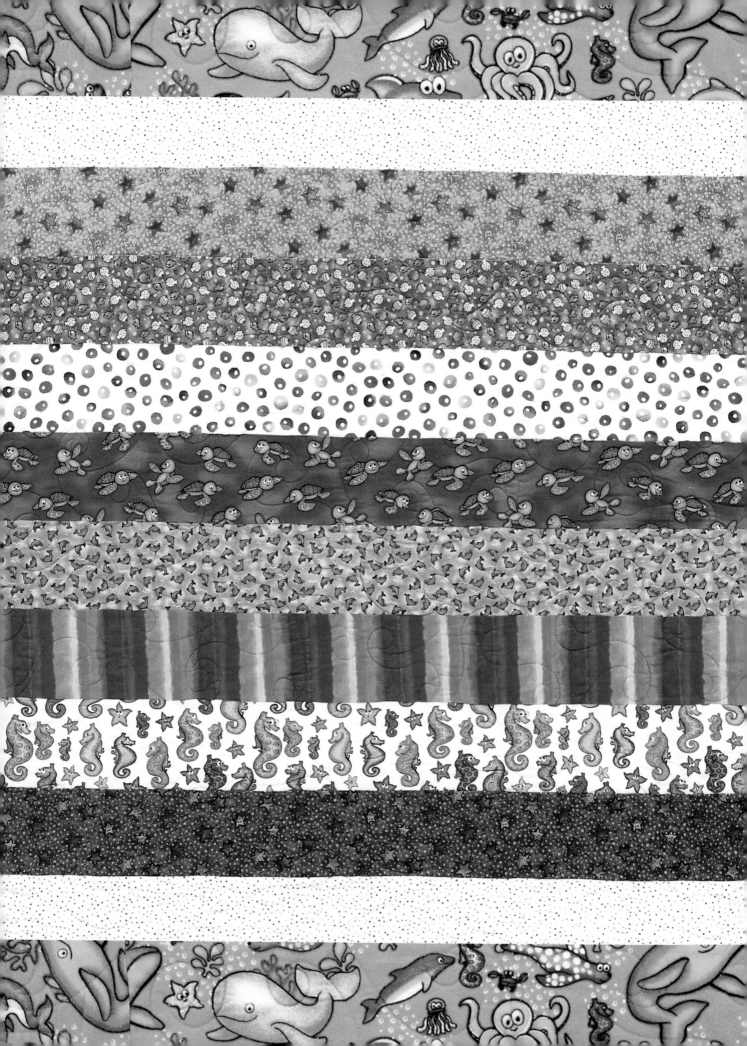

Contents

Introduction

I am a beginning quilter. In fact, I am a young beginning quilter. If you had told me two years ago that I would be writing a quilting book, I wouldn't have believed it. Before I started quilting in the fall of 2003, I didn't even sew! So, how does that make me qualified to write a book? Well, once I did start quilting, I was hooked, and I wanted others to see how fun and rewarding it is. I thought that by giving instructions for quilts designed and made by a beginner, maybe I would encourage others to try it themselves.

The average age of quilters today is 58. There is quite a gap between that and the age at which I started quilting—18. If my parents didn't own a quilt shop, I might not have gotten into this, but now that I have, I especially want younger people to know that quilting is like any other art form in which you can express your creativity. Color, texture, pattern, and every imaginable shape come together to make a quilt.

For me, the art isn't just in putting the pieces together and seeing a beautiful piece of work emerge; it's also in designing my own patterns. I get exactly what I want. All the patterns in this book have been tested at the quilt shop by other quilters. I get a lot of

Quilting is like any other art form in which

Let your *imagination*

compliments from people about how well written the instructions are, which is important no matter how long you've been quilting.

As you go through this book, you'll find a variety of projects that are excellent for any skill level. They're great projects for weekend retreats, for classes, or for teaching a beginner. The quilt-as-you-go projects are especially easy, and when you're done piecing, all you need to do is bind the edges! You'll find information about this method on page 14. Remember, all the projects were designed and made by a beginner, so you have nothing to be intimidated by. You CAN make

them! And if you make a mistake, it's OK. Just tell everyone you meant to do it that way. Basic quiltmaking and finishing instructions are also given on pages 9–12. These sections are intended as a review of what you hopefully learned in a basic quiltmaking class. Consult your local quilt shop for more-detailed instructions if needed.

Remember that you can always change the fabrics, colors, and size of a quilt or project to suit your desires. Use your creativity and have fun experimenting with your favorite fabrics. Let your imagination be your inspiration!

you can *express* your creativity.

be your inspiration!

Fabrics and Supplies

Quiltmakers have never had as many options as they do today. Just visit your local quilt shop and you'll find shelves loaded with fabrics and walls filled with an array of tools to make quilting quicker and easier. Here are some brief thoughts to remember when you're shopping.

Fabrics

Select the best fabrics you can afford and make sure they are 100% cotton. Good-quality cotton fabric will make your quilting experience more pleasant and produce a finished product that will last for generations.

I like to wash my fabrics before I cut out the pieces. This eliminates any shrinkage or bleeding that may occur after the quilt is finished. Wash your light and dark fabrics separately. Dry them in a dryer, using a warm to hot setting.

The fabric amounts given in the materials section for each project assume that the width of the fabric (measured from selvage to selvage) is at least 42" wide after washing and pressing, unless otherwise noted. In some cases, where only a small amount is needed, I call for a fat quarter. Fat quarters can vary in size depending on the original width of the fabric, but in general they are about 18" x 21".

Supplies

The following supplies should be on hand whenever you're quilting. As you become more experienced, you may find other tools and gadgets that you want to add to your sewing room.

Rotary cutter, self-healing mat, and clear acrylic rulers: There are several sizes and brands of cutters, mats, and rulers available for rotary cutting. If you don't already own these tools, start with an 18" x 24" mat, a 45mm rotary cutter, and a 6½" x 24" ruler.

Threads: Good-quality thread is as important as good-quality fabric. Cotton and cotton-covered polyester both work well for piecing. Select a thread color that blends with all of your fabrics, such as a neutral gray or beige.

Straight pins: Select rustproof pins with a fine shaft and sharp point. Pins with beaded heads are easier to handle and easier to find if you drop them.

Iron and ironing board: These are essential for pressing seams, finished blocks, and the quilt top and backing.

¼" presser foot: This is one of the tools that can help you achieve an accurate ¼" seam, which is essential to quiltmaking. Ask your sewing-machine dealer for the correct foot for your machine.

Seam ripper: Unfortunately, we all make mistakes. This tool will help you unsew your seam.

Fabric marker or chalk: No matter what you use to mark the fabric, be sure the mark can be removed from the fabric when you're finished. Test the marker on a piece of scrap fabric before you begin.

Quiltmaking Basics

This section will serve as a quick overview of the basic skills needed to make the quilts in this book. If you're a beginner, I hope you have taken a class from your local quilt shop that introduced you to the techniques presented here. If not, I encourage you to do so. There are also lots of good books available on quiltmaking techniques that can offer you information in greater detail.

Rotary Cutting

The first thing you do after washing and drying your fabrics is to cut the pieces. The quilts in this book all use rotary-cutting techniques to make this process quicker and more accurate than cutting with scissors. You will start by cutting strips. All strips are cut across the width of the fabric, from selvage to selvage. Some of these strips may be crosscut into smaller pieces. All the measurements given in the cutting instructions already include ¼"-wide seam allowances. Cut the pieces exactly as instructed and in the order given.

Note: Left-handers should do the reverse of what they see in the illustrations.

1. Fold the fabric in half lengthwise, wrong sides together. In all likelihood, the raw, cut edges will be uneven and the top and bottom layers will not line up, but the selvage edges should be aligned. Lay the fabric on the self-healing mat with the folded edge toward you.

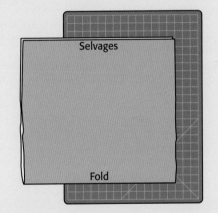

Quiltmaking is *fun* and rewarding. Use your creativity and have fun *experimenting* with your *favorite* fabrics.

2. Lay a 6½" x 24" ruler on the right-hand end of the fabric. Align a horizontal line of the ruler with the folded edge of the fabric. Position the ruler only as far in from the raw edges as needed to cut through all layers of fabric. Cut along the long edge of the ruler. Always cut away from yourself. Discard the cut piece.

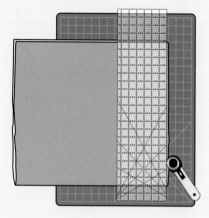

3. Rotate the fabric or mat so the straightened edge is to your left. Measuring from the straightened edge, cut strips to the width given in the pattern instructions. For example, if you need 2½"-wide strips, place the 2½" vertical line of the ruler on the straightened edge of the fabric. Cut along the right side of the ruler.

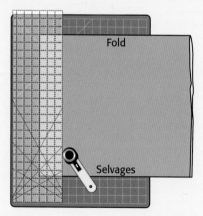

4. To cut squares and rectangles from strips, lay a folded strip on the rotary-cutting mat with the selvage ends to the right. Cut off and straighten the selvage ends of the folded strip by aligning a horizontal line of the ruler with the long edge of the folded strip like you did for the whole fabric piece. With the strip still folded, place the straightened edge to your left and then measure the required distance from the end of the strip to cut your pieces.

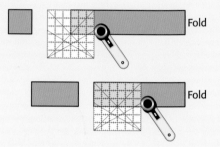

Machine Piecing

When you sew your pieces together, always be sure to place the pieces right sides together and align the raw edges. To help with accuracy, always pin your pieces together. Pins should be placed at the beginning and end of a new seam and wherever seams join. In between those points, place pins 1½" to 2" apart.

It is important that all of your seams measure ¼" wide; otherwise, the seams might not match and your blocks may end up being a different size than what they are supposed to be according to the instructions. This in turn will affect how everything fits together.

There are several ways to achieve an accurate ¼" seam. If your machine has a ¼" presser foot available, try using it. If possible, the needle position can also be adjusted. Or, you can use a ruler to measure ¼" to the right of the needle. Place a piece of tape or

"Quiltmakers have *never* had as many *options* as they do today."

FUSSY CUTTING

If you want to cut out a particular motif from your fabric, this can be done with a technique called fussy cutting. Rather than cutting strips first, position the ruler over the individual motif and cut it out separately. Be sure you allow for the ¼" seam allowance on each edge. The following examples show a square of fabric that was fussy cut and a square from the same fabric that was not fussy cut.

Fussy cut

Not fussy cut

moleskin at this position and guide your fabric along it. With any of these methods, you should check to be sure your seams are accurate. To do this, cut three 2" x 6" strips of fabric. Sew the strips together along the long edges, and then press the seams. The center strip should measure 1½" wide. If not, make adjustments in your needle position or realign your tape until the correct width is achieved.

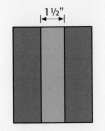

You can save time and thread by chain piecing. This is simply a process in which you feed the pieces through the machine one after the other without stopping after each piece to cut the threads. To chain piece, sew the first pair of pieces from cut edge to cut edge. Stop sewing at the end of the seam, but don't cut the thread. Feed the next pair of pieces under the presser foot, leaving about ¼" of space from the first pair of pieces. Continue feeding pieces through the machine in this manner until you have a chain of pieces. Remove the chain from the machine and clip the threads between the pieces.

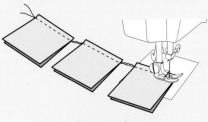

Chain piecing

Strip Units

For many of the quilts in this book, you will be sewing two or more strips together along the long edges and then cutting these joined strips into smaller segments. The segments will be used to make larger units or blocks.

1. Cut the strips from the required fabrics and sew them together along the long edges as indicated in the project instructions.

2. Lay the strip unit on the ironing board so the seams are perpendicular to the length of the board as shown. Press the seams open or as indicated in the instructions. Be careful not to stretch the strips as you press.

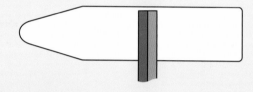

3. Refer to "Rotary Cutting" on page 9 to straighten one end of the strip unit and then cut it into smaller units as detailed in the instructions.

Assembling the Quilt Top

After your quilt blocks are complete, arrange them according to the instructions and illustrations for each project. Some may have a particular order, and some you can arrange any way you like. Sew the blocks together in horizontal rows unless instructed otherwise. Press the seams in opposite directions from row to row so that the seams will fit together nicely when sewing. You can also press seams open for less bulk. Sew the rows together, pressing the seams in one direction.

Adding Borders

The projects in this book use the straight-cut border technique. Refer to the cutting instructions for each project to determine the number of border strips needed.

1. Measure the length of the quilt top through the center. Cut two border strips to fit this measurement, piecing strips together and trimming as necessary to achieve strips of the desired length. Then mark the center of the quilt-top sides and border strips.

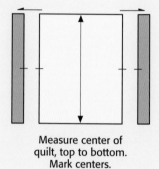

Measure center of
quilt, top to bottom.
Mark centers.

2. With right sides together, pin the border strips to the sides of the quilt top, matching center marks and easing as necessary. Sew the border strips in place. Press the seams toward the border unless instructed otherwise.

3. Measure the width of the quilt top through the center, including the border strips just added. Cut two border strips to fit this measurement, piecing and trimming as necessary. Mark the center of the quilt-top sides and border strips.

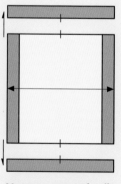

Measure center of quilt,
side to side, including borders.
Mark centers.

4. With right sides together, pin the border strips to the top and bottom edges of the quilt top, matching center marks and easing as necessary. Sew the border strips in place. Press the seams toward the border unless instructed otherwise.

Finishing Techniques

It's a great feeling to have your quilt top finished, but I guarantee that having the whole quilt done is an even greater rush. This section will get you through the final stages and on your way to feeling fine!

Note: If your project uses the quilt-as-you-go method, skip to "Binding" on page 15.

Preparing the Layers

When your quilt top is complete, measure the width and the length. You will need batting and backing pieces that are at least 4" larger on all sides than your quilt top, especially if your project will be quilted on a long-arm machine. If necessary, cut and piece your backing fabric so it is large enough, or purchase extra-wide backing fabric so your backing can be cut in one piece. Extra-wide backings can range from 60" wide up to 120" wide. If you piece your backing, press seams open or to one side.

1. Lay your backing, wrong side up, on a flat surface, making sure there are no wrinkles. Secure the edges with masking tape. Smooth the batting over the backing.

2. Center your pressed quilt top, right side up, over the batting. Smooth out any wrinkles and keep the edges parallel to the backing.

3. Use curved basting pins or basting spray to baste your three layers together. Pins should be placed 3" to 4" apart over the entire quilt, starting in the center and working outward. *Don't baste the layers together if your quilt is going to be quilted on a long-arm machine.*

Quilting

All of the quilts in this book were quilted on a Gammill long-arm machine by my mother, except for the quilt-as-you-go projects. Read the hints in "Long-Arm Quilting" below if you intend to use this method. The instructions for the quilt-as-you-go method are on page 14.

You also can choose to quilt your project by hand or machine. Whichever method you choose to use, always select a design that will enhance your quilt. This can be anything from quilting in the ditch to outline quilting to using a quilting stencil. Be sure to start in the middle and work out to the edges to prevent any bunching. When you're done quilting, trim the batting and backing even with the quilt top, and make sure the corners are square.

Long-Arm Quilting

Here are a few helpful hints to consider when taking your projects to a long-arm quilter, but always be sure to ask your quilter about personal preferences.

- Check with your long-arm quilter to see what his or her schedule is. Many are booked months out, so try to plan ahead and make an appointment early. Be thinking of design and thread choice before making an appointment.

- If your project contains materials other than quilting cotton, such as denim, fleece, or T-shirt fabric, make sure you tell your quilter. Some quilters will not quilt through these fabrics or will charge you an additional fee to do so.

- Ask about batting and backing preferences. Some quilters will not work on projects that use sheets, fleece, or other materials for backings.

- Batting and backing should be cut about 4" to 6" larger on all sides than your quilt top. Have your backing sewn together and make sure it is square. The best way to square up your backing is to rip your fabric along the lengthwise and crosswise grainlines before you piece the backing together. Use your scissors to make a small snip to begin the tear along the edge you wish to rip, and then proceed to tear the fabric. When you rip along the lengthwise grain, make your snip just inside the selvages so that they will be removed.

- There is no need to baste your top, batting, and backing together. The top and backing are loaded on separate rollers.

- Cut away any loose threads. They can cause the machine to skip stitches and may show through your top or backing.

- Check for any open seams on the quilt top and repair any that need fixing. The quilting machine's foot can get caught and tear your top.

- Don't add any embellishments, such as buttons, trims, and pins, to your quilt top until after it has been quilted.

- Press the quilt top and backing and hang them over a hanger or in a hanging bag.

- Be prompt in picking up your quilt when the quilter is done.

Quilt-as-You-Go Method

"Quilt as you go" is a method that allows you to quilt your project at the same time that you're piecing it together. When you're finished, all you need to do is bind the edges! You won't see any quilting stitches on the top of your project, but you'll see the thread on the back, so use a thread that will blend in with your backing fabric. You can use the ¼" foot for sewing the pieces, or you can use your walking foot, which helps keep the layers from shifting. Practice on some scrap pieces of batting and fabric to see which is easier for you to sew with. The project instructions will tell you what size to cut your batting and backing pieces.

The quilt-as-you-go patterns can also be made with traditional piecing methods. Just skip the basting steps and sew the top pieces together as instructed in the pattern.

To quilt as you go, follow these steps.

1. Baste your batting to the *wrong* side of your backing. Fusible batting is excellent for this method, but you can use any technique you prefer for basting. Also, the thinner the batting, the easier the sewing will be.

2. With the batting facing up, measure each side to find and mark the center, both horizontally and vertically. Use a fabric marker and a ruler to draw a line connecting the center points on each side and the points on the top and bottom edges.

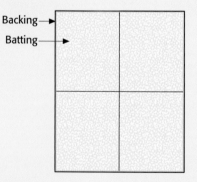

3. Follow the project instructions to position the first piece on the batting and pin it in place. Lay the next piece, right sides together, over the first piece as indicated in the instructions, and stitch through all of the layers. Press the piece out. Continue adding pieces in this manner, stitching through all of the layers and then pressing the piece out before adding the next piece.

Binding

Fabric requirements listed in this book for binding are based on using straight-grain binding strips cut 2¼" wide and stitched to the outside edges of the quilt with ¼"-wide seams. Simply purchase more fabric if you would like a wider binding. If you prefer bias binding, refer to "Bias Binding" on page 17.

1. Cut the number of binding strips indicated in the cutting instructions for your project. Cut the strips from selvage to selvage.

2. Stitch the strips together as shown to make one long strip. Trim the seam allowances to ¼". Press the seams open.

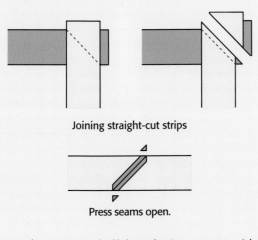

Joining straight-cut strips

Press seams open.

3. Press the strip in half lengthwise, wrong sides together. Press carefully, keeping the raw edges even.

4. Place the folded binding in the middle of any side of your quilt. Line up the raw edges of the binding with the edge of the quilt top. Pin the binding in place from the binding end to the first corner. Measure ¼" (or whatever your desired seam allowance is) from the corner and mark the point with a pin as shown. Start sewing 6" from the beginning tail of your binding strip. End

sewing at the pin; backstitch. Remove your project from the sewing machine.

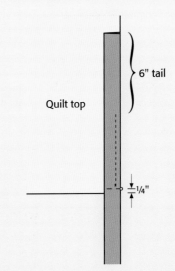

Quilt top

6" tail

¼"

5. Turn the quilt like you would for sewing down the next side. Fold the binding up at a 45° angle. Hold the fold in place, and then fold the binding back down so the edges are aligned with the quilt top as shown. Pin the binding in place, inserting another pin ¼" from the lower corner. Stitch the binding in place, beginning at the top edge and stopping when you reach the pin at the lower corner. Repeat this process at each corner.

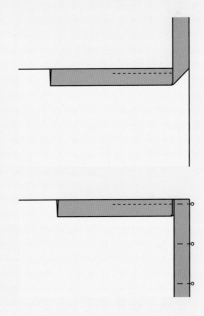

6. Stop sewing about 6" from the beginning tail of your binding strip. Trim the end tail of the binding so it overlaps the beginning tail by 2¼" (or whatever width your binding strips were cut).

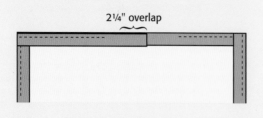

2¼" overlap

7. Open the folds of both tails and overlap them, right sides together, as shown; pin in place to secure. Draw a diagonal line as shown (the solid line).

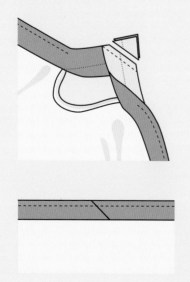

Pin ends together.
Draw diagonal line.

8. Sew on the marked line. Check to make sure the binding fits along the unbound edge, and then trim ¼" from the stitching line. Finger-press the seam open. Refold the binding in half and finish sewing it to the quilt top.

9. Wrap the binding over the edge of the quilt so it covers the stitching. Hand stitch the binding in place with a blind hem stitch, mitering and stitching down the corners.

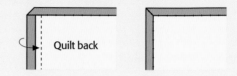

Quilt back

Adding a Label

Every quilting project should have a label. Labels can tell a lot about where a quilt came from. You can make your own quilt label from muslin, solid white fabric, or fabric from your project. Use a textile marker or permanent pen or marker to write on your labels. You can also purchase premade labels or make them on your computer and print them out on fabric sheets. Or, if you own an embroidery machine or know someone who does, you can make your own that way too.

Try to include at least the following information on your label: your first and last name and the name of anyone else involved in piecing or quilting the quilt, the year the quilt was started and completed, and the city and state in which the quilt was made. If possible, you may want to include a little message that tells for whom the quilt was made and the occasion.

Hand stitch your label to a lower corner of the quilt backing.

> ### STORAGE DOS AND DON'TS
> - **Don't** store your quilts in plastic. This can cause fibers to break down faster.
> - **Do** store your quilts in pillowcases or wrapped in cloth.
> - **Don't** store or display your quilts in direct sunlight. The sun can fade fabric greatly in a short amount of time.
> - **Don't** store your quilts in an attic or a damp basement.
> - **Do** refold your quilts every few months so that the creases don't become permanent.

BIAS BINDING

Binding a quilt with bias-cut binding is done in much the same manner as with straight-cut binding; the strips are cut the same width but they are cut on the bias grain of the fabric. You will probably need more fabric than the amount indicated in the materials list if you decide to use bias binding. To determine the yardage needed, measure the perimeter of the quilt. Using a calculator, multiply this measurement (in inches) by the width of the strip (2.25"). Press the square root button. The number shown will be the size of the square you need to cut from the fabric. For good measure, add 2" to 3" to the square size. Now you are ready to cut the strips.

1. Press the square in half diagonally. It doesn't matter if right or wrong sides are together. Fold the triangle in half again as shown.

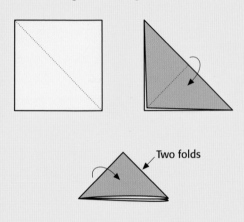

Two folds

2. Turn the triangle as shown. Lay a small, square ruler on the triangle, close to but not aligned with the left edge. Keep the bottom edge of the ruler aligned with the bottom edge of the triangle. While you're holding the ruler in place, butt a long ruler against the left side of the square ruler. Now, hold the long ruler in place and remove the square ruler. Cut along the right edge of the long ruler to remove the folded edges of the triangle.

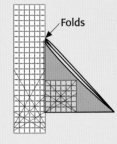

Folds

Remove both folds.

3. Measuring from the newly cut edge, cut as many 2¼"-wide strips across the triangle as possible.

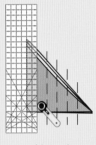

Cut bias strips.

4. Stitch the strips together as shown to make one long strip. Trim the seam allowances to ¼". Press the seams open.

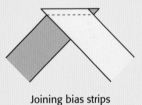

Joining bias strips

5. Press the strip in half lengthwise, wrong sides together. Trim the beginning ends so they are straight and not at an angle.

6. Follow steps 4–9 of "Binding" on page 15 to bind the quilt edges with the strips.

The Projects

Boxed In

Flutterby Wishes

Heaven's Bliss

Inside Out

Flying KoKo

Inspiration Point

Quick-Strip Baby Quilt

Peaceful Haven

Pillowcase

Spun Rail

Twisted Strips

Boxed In

This table runner is *fast* and *easy* to make when you use the quilt-as-you-go method. And it goes together even more quickly when you use fusible batting!

Finished table runner size: 34" x 18"

Materials

Yardages are based on 42"-wide fabrics.

- ¾ yard of main print for center squares and outer border
- ¾ yard of coordinating print for sashing, inner border, outer border corner squares, and binding
- ¾ yard of fabric for backing
- 26" x 42" piece of batting

Cutting

All measurements include ¼"-wide seam allowances.

From the main print, cut:

1 strip, 6½" x 42"; crosscut the strip into
    3 squares, 6½" x 6½"

3 strips, 4½" x 42"

From the coordinating print, cut:

3 strips, 2½" x 42"; crosscut 1 strip into
    4 rectangles, 2½" x 6½"

1 strip, 4½" x 42"; crosscut the strip into
    4 squares, 4½" x 4½"

3 strips, 2¼" x 42"

From the backing, cut:

1 rectangle, 26" x 42"

Assembling the Table Runner

1. Refer to "Quilt-as-You-Go Method" on page 14 to baste the batting to your backing. If you're using fusible batting, follow the manufacturer's instructions to adhere the batting to the wrong side of the backing. Mark the horizontal and vertical center lines on the batting. Always have the table runner facing you as shown, with the batting right side up.

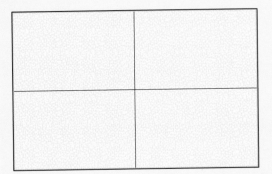

2. Mark dashed lines 3¼" above and below the horizontal centerline as shown.

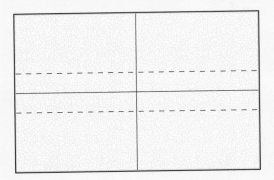

3. Mark dashed lines 3¼" to the left and right of the vertical centerline as shown, ending the lines where they intersect with the horizontal dashed lines to form a square.

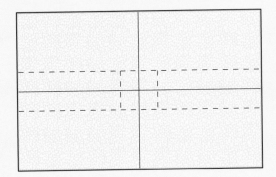

4. Place one main print square, right side up, in the square that was formed by the horizontal and vertical dashed lines. Pin the square in place, inserting the pins so they're perpendicular to the square edges.

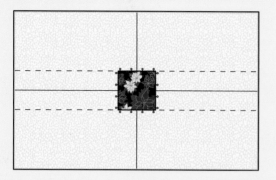

5. With right sides together, place a coordinating print 2½" x 6½" rectangle on the sides of the square as shown. Be sure the top and bottom edges of the strips align with the dashed horizontal lines. Stitch through all the layers, removing the pins before you stitch over them. Press the strips out.

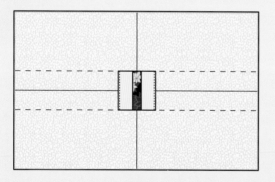

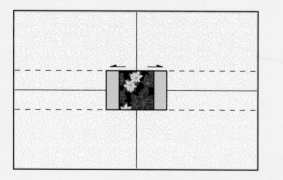

6. Sew a main print square to the long, raw edges of the coordinating print rectangles, followed by the remaining two coordinating print rectangles, as shown. Again, be sure to use the dashed horizontal lines to position the pieces, and press each piece out before adding the next piece.

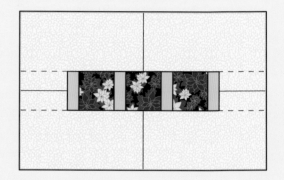

7. Refer to "Adding Borders" on page 12 to measure the center section for the inner top and bottom borders. From the remaining coordinating print 2½" x 42" strips, cut two pieces to the length measured and sew them to the top and bottom edges of the center section. Press the pieces out.

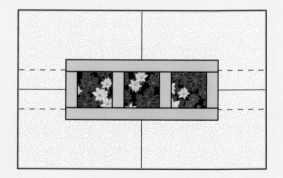

8. Refer to "Adding Borders" on page 12 to measure the sides of the table runner top for the outer side borders. From one of the main print 4½" x 42" strips, cut two pieces to the length measured. Sew a coordinating print square to the ends of each of these pieces. Press the seams

toward the main print, and then set the pieced side borders aside.

9. Measure the table runner top for the outer top and bottom borders. From the remaining main print 4½" x 42" strips, cut two pieces to the length measured and sew them to the top and bottom edges of the table runner top. Press the pieces out.

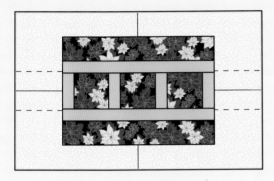

10. Sew the pieced side borders from step 8 to the sides of the table runner top, matching the seams. Press the pieces out.

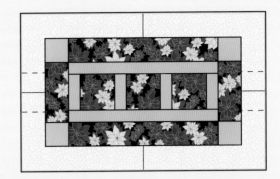

11. Press the completed top and trim the excess batting and backing even with the edges.

12. Refer to "Binding" on page 15 to bind the edges with the coordinating print 2¼"-wide strips. Refer to "Adding a Label" on page 16 to add a label to the back.

As quickly as this table runner makes up, you can make several in different color options in no time at all. This classic red-and-white combination would be ideal for a romantic Valentine dinner with your sweetheart.

Pick a *fabulous* print and showcase it in the large center square of the blocks that form this quilt. Two strips *border* each side of the squares but appear as sashing in the finished quilt.

Finished quilt size: 56" x 72" · Finished block size: 16" x 16"

Materials

Yardages are based on 42"-wide fabrics.

- 1⅝ yards of multicolored fabric for block centers
- 1¼ yards of blue fabric for block setting corner-stones and border
- ⅝ yard *each* of green, cream, tan, and gold fabrics for block border strips
- 4 yards of fabric for backing
- ⅝ yard of fabric for binding
- 64" x 80" piece of batting

Cutting

All measurements include ¼"-wide seam allowances.

From the blue fabric, cut:

4 strips, 1½" x 42"; crosscut the strips into
    8 rectangles, 1½" x 20"

7 strips, 4½" x 42"

From the green fabric, cut:

1 strip, 14½" x 42"; crosscut the strip into:
    1 rectangle, 12½" x 20"
    1 rectangle, 14½" x 20"

From the tan fabric, cut:

1 strip, 14½" x 42"; crosscut the strip into:
    1 rectangle, 12½" x 20"
    1 rectangle, 14½" x 20"

From the multicolored fabric, cut:

4 strips, 12½" x 42"; crosscut the strips into
    12 squares, 12½" x 12½"

From the gold fabric, cut:

10 strips, 1½" x 42"; crosscut the strips into:
    12 rectangles, 1½" x 12½"
    12 rectangles, 1½" x 14½"

From the cream fabric, cut:

10 strips, 1½" x 42"; crosscut the strips into:
    12 rectangles, 1½" x 12½"
    12 rectangles, 1½" x 14½"

From the binding fabric, cut:

7 strips, 2¼" x 42"

Assembling the Blocks

1. Sew a blue 1½" x 20" rectangle to both long edges of the green 12½" x 20" rectangle and the tan 12½" x 20" rectangle as shown to make strip sets. Press the seams toward the green and tan rectangles. From each strip set, cut 12 segments, 1½" wide. Set the units aside.

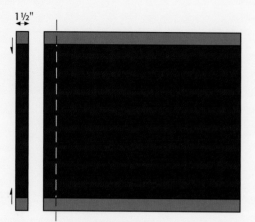

1½"

Make 1 strip set.
Cut 12 segments.

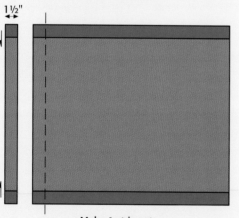

1½"

Make 1 strip set.
Cut 12 segments.

2. Repeat step 1 to sew a blue 1½" x 20" rectangle to both long edges of the green 14½" x 20" strip and the tan 14½" x 20" strip. Cut each strip set into 12 segments, 1½" wide. Set the units aside.

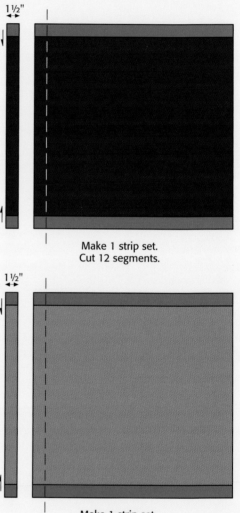

1½"

Make 1 strip set.
Cut 12 segments.

1½"

Make 1 strip set.
Cut 12 segments.

3. Sew a gold 1½" x 12½" rectangle to any side of each multicolored 12½" square. Sew a cream 1½" x 12½" rectangle to the opposite side of each square. *If your square was cut from a directional print, randomly place the rectangles on different sides of each square.* Press the seams away from the center square.

4. Sew a green-and-blue unit from step 1 to one of the remaining sides of each square as shown, matching seams. Sew a tan-and-blue unit from step 1 to the remaining side of each square as shown, matching seams. Press the seams away from the center square.

5. Sew a gold 1½" x 14½" rectangle to each block on the edge opposite the first gold rectangle. Repeat with the cream 1½" x 14½" rectangles. Press the seams away from the center square.

6. Sew a green-and-blue unit from step 2 and a tan-and-blue unit from step 2 to each block on the edge opposite the step 1 units, matching seams. Press the seams away from the center square. The blocks should measure 16½" x 16½".

Assembling and Finishing the Quilt

1. Refer to the quilt assembly diagram to arrange the blocks into four rows of three blocks each, rotating the blocks as desired to form a pleasing layout. Sew the blocks in each row together and then sew the rows together.

2. Refer to "Adding Borders" on page 12 to sew the 4½"-wide blue strips to your quilt top.

3. Refer to "Finishing Techniques" on page 13 for specific instructions on layering, quilting, and binding the quilt, and adding a label to the back. The quilt shown was quilted on a long-arm machine using the Hearts and Loops pantograph designed by Linda Taylor of Linda's Electric Quilters (www.lequilters.com).

Quilt assembly

Colorful girlish prints set the tone for fun in this quilt made by Shirley Snyder for her granddaughter, Madeline Dostal.

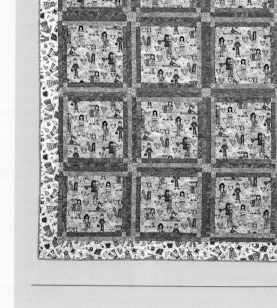

Flying KoKo

Use a *favorite* fabric for the center panel of this quick-and-easy quilt. Simply border it with strips of *colorful* fabrics and easy-to-make flying-geese units and you'll be snuggling under it in no time at all.

Finished quilt size: 52" x 69"

Materials

Yardages are based on 42"-wide fabrics.

- 1¾ yards of black fabric for flying-geese backgrounds, square-in-a-square units, and border
- 1 yard of novelty print for center panel and square-in-a-square units
- ⅝ yard *each* of orange, yellow, and green batik fabrics for strips and flying-geese bodies
- 3⅝ yards of fabric for backing
- ⅝ yard of fabric for binding
- 60" x 77" piece of batting

Cutting

From the novelty print, cut:

1 rectangle, 25½" x 40½"

2 fussy-cut squares, 4½" x 4½". Cut out the squares so that when they are standing on their points, rather than on a flat side, the motif is straight.

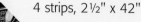

From the orange batik, cut:

4 strips, 2½" x 42"

1 strip, 5¼" x 42"; crosscut the strip into 3 squares, 5¼" x 5¼"

From the yellow batik, cut:

4 strips, 2½" x 42"

1 strip, 5¼" x 42"; crosscut the strip into 3 squares, 5¼" x 5¼"

From the green batik, cut:

4 strips, 2½" x 42"

1 strip, 5¼" x 42"; crosscut the strip into 3 squares, 5¼" x 5¼"

From the black fabric, cut:

1 strip, 2⅜" x 42"; crosscut the strip into 8 squares, 2⅜" x 2⅜"

3 strips, 2⅞" x 42"; crosscut the strips into 36 squares, 2⅞" x 2⅞"

7 strips, 6½" x 42"

From the binding fabric, cut:

7 strips, 2¼" x 42"

Assembling the Quilt

1. Sew one orange, one yellow, and one green 2½" x 42" strip together as shown. Press the seams toward the green strips. Make four. Trim each unit to 6½" x 40½". Set the strip units aside.

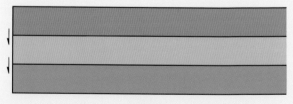

Make 4.

2. Use a fabric marker or chalk to draw a diagonal line from corner to corner on the wrong side of all of the black 2⅜" and 2⅞" squares.

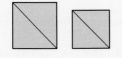

3. Place a marked 2⅜" square on opposite corners of one novelty print 4½" square as shown, right sides together. The squares will overlap slightly in the center; pin in place. Sew on the marked lines. Cut ¼" from the sewn line; press the seams open. Repeat on the remaining corners. Make two. The square-in-a-square units should measure 4½" x 4½". Set the units aside.

Make 2.

4. With right sides together, place a marked 2⅞" square on opposite corners of one orange 5¼" square as shown so that the marked lines meet. The black squares will overlap slightly in the center; pin in place. Sew ¼" from each side of the diagonal line.

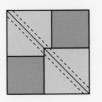

5. Cut on the marked line. Press the seams open.

6. Place another marked black 2⅞" square, right sides together, on the large triangle of each of the two resulting pieces as shown; pin in place. Sew ¼" from each side of the marked line.

7. Cut on the marked line of each square and press the seams open. Trim off the "mouse ears" that extend beyond each of the four resulting flying-geese units. Each unit should measure 2½" x 4½".

8. Repeat steps 4–7 with the remaining orange, yellow, and green 5¼" squares. You should have a total of 36 flying-geese units (12 of each color).

9. Sew one orange, one yellow, and one green flying-geese unit together as shown. Make 12.

Make 12.

10. Sew six flying-geese units and one square-in-a-square unit together as shown. Make two. The pieced strips should measure 4½" x 40½".

Make 2.

11. Sew a strip unit from step 1 to each side of the pieced strips from step 10 as shown. Make two.

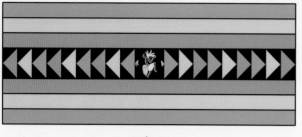

Make 2.

12. Refer to the quilt assembly diagram to sew the units from step 11 to the novelty print 25½" x 40½" rectangle as shown.

13. Refer to "Adding Borders" on page 12 to sew the 6½"-wide black strips to your quilt top.

14. Refer to "Finishing Techniques" on page 13 for specific instructions on layering, quilting, and binding the quilt, and adding a label to the back.

Quilt assembly

A retro drive-in movie print is the perfect choice for wrapping up in to watch your favorite flicks.

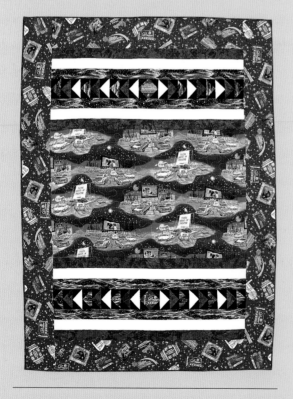

Heaven's Bliss

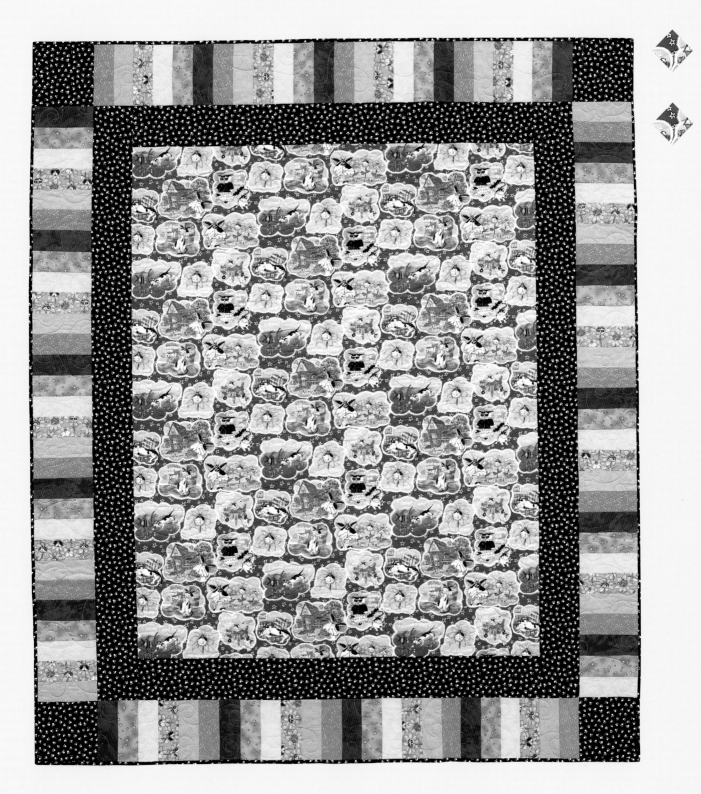

Do you have a *special* fabric that you just can't bear to cut into? This quilt offers you a large space to show it off in all its *glory*.

Finished quilt size: 60" x 70"

Materials

Yardages are based on 42"-wide fabrics.

- 1⅝ yards of novelty print for center panel
- 1⅛ yards of black print for inner border and corner squares
- ⅜ yard *each* of 6 assorted prints for pieced outer border
- 4 yards of fabric for backing
- ⅝ yard of fabric for binding
- 68" x 78" piece of batting

Cutting

All measurements include ¼"-wide seam allowances.

From the novelty print, cut:

1 rectangle, 40½" x 50½"

From the black print, cut:

6 strips, 4½" x 42"

1 strip, 6½" x 42"; crosscut the strip into 4 squares, 6½" x 6½"

From *each* of the 6 assorted prints, cut:

3 strips (18 total), 2½" x 42"

From the binding fabric, cut:

7 strips, 2¼" x 42"

Assembling the Quilt

1. Refer to "Adding Borders" on page 12 to sew the black 4½"-wide strips to the center panel as shown.

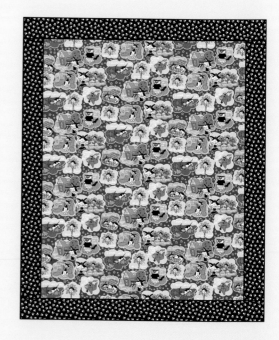

2. Sew one of each of the assorted print 2½" x 42" strips together along the long edges in an order pleasing to you. Make three. From the strip sets, cut 18 segments, 6½" wide.

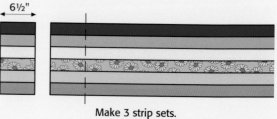

Make 3 strip sets.
Cut 18 segments.

3. To make the side borders, sew five segments together side by side. Make two. Remove one strip from each pieced border strip.

Remove.

Side border.
Make 2.

4. To make the top and bottom borders, sew four segments together side by side. Make two. Sew a black 6½" square to the ends of each pieced strip.

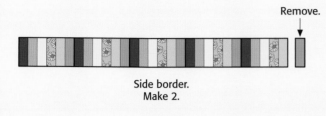

Top/bottom border.
Make 2.

5. Sew the side border strips to the sides of the quilt top, reversing the direction of one strip to vary the color placement. Repeat with the top and bottom border strips.

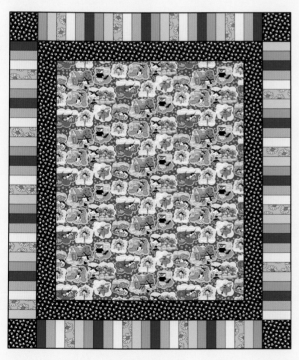

Quilt assembly

6. Refer to "Finishing Techniques" on page 13 for specific instructions on layering, quilting, and binding the quilt, and adding a label to the back.

The center panel of this quilt design is a great place to feature a large-scale print.

Make any holiday more cheerful with this *whimsical* wall hanging. Just change the print to match the theme and you're ready to *celebrate!*

Finished quilt size: 31" x 41"

Materials

Yardages are based on 42"-wide fabrics.

- ⅝ yard of focus fabric for quilt center
- ⅝ yard of novelty print for outer border*
- ⅜ yard of dark blue print for inner border
- ¼ yard *each* of red, blue, white, and green prints for checkerboard sashing
- 1½ yards of fabric for backing
- ½ yard of fabric for binding
- 39" x 49" piece of batting

*Yardage is based on a nondirectional print. You will need 1½ yards if you choose a directional print.

Cutting

All measurements include ¼"-wide seam allowances.

From the focus fabric, cut:

1 strip, 8½" x 42"; crosscut the strip into 2 rectangles, 8½" x 18½"

1 rectangle, 6½" x 18½"

From *each* of the red, blue, white, and green prints, cut:

2 strips (8 total), 1½" x 42"

From the dark blue print, cut:

4 strips, 2" x 42"

From the novelty print, cut:

4 strips, 4½" x 42". For directional prints, cut all of the strips so that the pattern is going in the same direction when the strips are applied to the quilt top.

From the binding fabric, cut:

5 strips, 2¼" x 42"

Making the Checkerboard Units

1. Sew one blue and one white 1½" x 42" strip together along the long edges to make a strip set. Make two. Press the seams open. Crosscut the strip sets into 51 segments, 1½" wide.

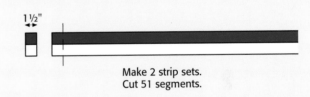

1½"

**Make 2 strip sets.
Cut 51 segments.**

2. Repeat step 1 with the red and green 1½" x 42" strips.

1½"

**Make 2 strip sets.
Cut 51 segments.**

3. Sew a blue-and-white segment to a red-and-green segment as shown to make the two variations of four-patch units. Pay close attention to the placement of the colors in each unit. Make 20 of each variation. Press the seams open. Set the remaining segments aside for use later.

Make 20.   Make 20.

4. Sew five of each of the two variations of four-patch units together as shown. Make four. Press the seams open. The rows should measure 2½" x 20½". Set the rows aside.

Make 4.

5. Sew the leftover segments from step 3 into rows as shown. Make the amount indicated for each row. Press the seams open.

Make 4.

Make 1.   Make 1.

Assembling and Finishing the Quilt

1. Sew the focus fabric rectangles and the checkerboard rows together as shown. Pay close attention to color placement. The quilt top should now measure 20½" x 30½".

2. Refer to "Adding Borders" on page 12 to sew the 2"-wide dark blue strips to your quilt top, followed by the 4½"-wide novelty print strips.

Quilt assembly

3. Refer to "Finishing Techniques" on page 13 for specific instructions on layering, quilting, and binding the quilt, and adding a label to the back.

Decorate your favorite haunt with a Halloween-themed print.

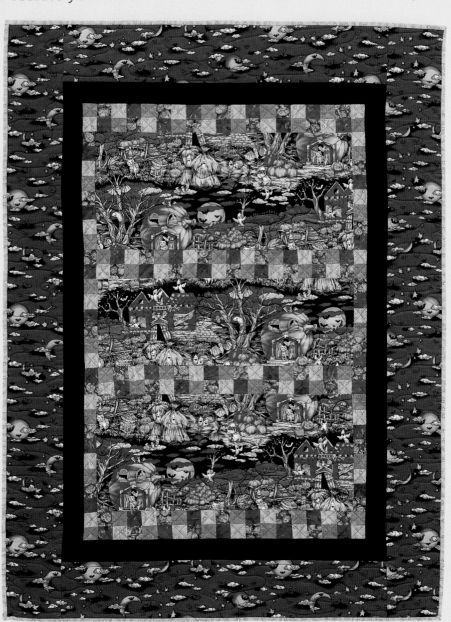

Inspiration Point

Talk about easy! Using the *quilt-as-you-go* technique, you can start this project after breakfast and be ready to bind the edges by lunchtime. The finished quilt makes a *great* wall hanging or table topper.

Finished quilt size: 40" x 40"

Materials

Yardages are based on 42"-wide fabrics.

- ¾ yard of red print for wide borders
- ⅝ yard of holly print for medium borders
- ⅝ yard of cardinal print for center square and corner triangles
- ⅜ yard of green print for narrow borders
- 1½ yards of fabric for backing
- ½ yard of fabric for binding
- 48" x 48" piece of batting

Cutting

All measurements include ¼"-wide seam allowances.

From the cardinal print, cut:

1 strip, 15⅛" x 42"; crosscut the strip into:
>   2 squares, 15⅛" x 15⅛"*
>   1 square, 8½" x 8½"**

If you're using a nondirectional print, cut each square once diagonally to yield 4 triangles. If you're using a directional print, lay both squares right side up so the print reads correctly as it faces you. Cut one square once diagonally from the upper-left corner to the lower-right corner; cut the remaining square from the lower-left corner to the upper-right corner.

**If you're using a directional print, fussy cut the square so that when it is standing on its point, rather than on a flat side, the motif is straight.*

From the green print, cut:

5 strips, 1½" x 42"; crosscut the strips into:
>   2 strips, 1½" x 8½"
>   2 strips, 1½" x 10½"
>   2 strips, 1½" x 28½"
>   2 strips, 1½" x 30½"

From the holly print, cut:

6 strips, 2½" x 42"; crosscut the strips into:
>   2 strips, 2½" x 10½"
>   2 strips, 2½" x 14½"
>   2 strips, 2½" x 30½"
>   2 strips, 2½" x 34½"

From the red print, cut:

6 strips, 3½" x 42"; crosscut the strips into:
>   2 strips, 3½" x 14½"
>   2 strips, 3½" x 20½"
>   2 strips, 3½" x 34½"
>   2 strips, 3½" x 40½"

From the binding fabric, cut:

5 strips, 2¼" x 42"

Assembling the Quilt

1. Piece the backing fabric to create a 48" x 48" square.

2. Refer to "Quilt-as-You-Go Method" on page 14 to baste the batting to your backing. If you're using fusible batting, follow the manufacturer's instructions to adhere the batting to the wrong side of the backing. Mark the horizontal and vertical centerlines on the batting.

3. Place the cardinal print 8½" square, right side up, in the center of the batting, lining up the points of the square with the centerlines. Pin the square in place, inserting the pins so they're perpendicular to the square edges.

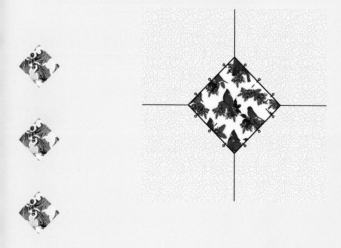

4. With right sides together, place a green 1½" x 8½" strip on opposite sides of the center square as shown. Pin the strips in place and sew through all of the layers. Press the strips out.

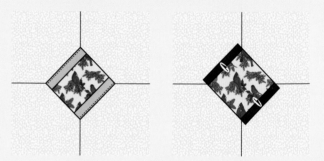

5. Sew a green 1½" x 10½" strip to the remaining sides of the center square; press the strips out.

6. Repeat steps 4 and 5 with the following strips in the order listed:

   2½" x 10½" holly strips
   2½" x 14½" holly strips
   3½" x 14½" red strips
   3½" x 20½" red strips

   The pieced center should now measure 20½" x 20½".

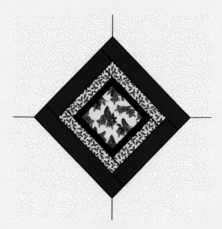

7. Sew a cardinal print triangle to each side of the quilt center as shown. If you're using a directional print, make sure to position the triangles so they are all facing the same direction. The quilt center should now measure 28½" x 28½".

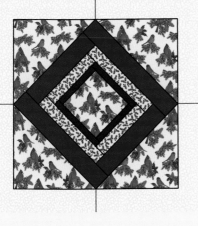

8. Repeat steps 4 and 5 to add the remaining strips in the order listed:

   1½" x 28½" green strips
   1½" x 30½" green strips
   2½" x 30½" holly strips
   2½" x 34½" holly strips
   3½" x 34½" red strips
   3½" x 40½" red strips

9. Press the completed top and trim off the excess batting and backing even with the edges. Refer to "Binding" on page 15 to bind the edges with the 2¼"-wide binding strips. Refer to "Adding a Label" on page 16 to add a label.

Pastel fabrics inspire a totally different mood.

Peaceful Haven

This quilt offers a little more challenge when picking out fabrics, but the sewing is still *simple*. Make your fabric selection easier by starting with a coordinating group from one manufacturer, and then adding from other fabric lines as necessary for the *right* mix.

Finished quilt size: 72" x 86" • Finished block size: 16" x 16"

Materials

Yardages are based on 42"-wide fabrics.

- ½ yard *each* of 4 different colors of the same print for pieced blocks
- 1⅞ yards of main print for plain blocks and third border
- 1⅞ yards of multicolored print for outer border
- ⅞ yard of medium blue tone-on-tone print for second border
- ⅞ yard of dark blue print for fourth border and binding
- ¾ yard of purple tone-on-tone print for first border
- 5½ yards of fabric for backing
- 80" x 94" piece of batting

Cutting

All measurements include ¼"-wide seam allowances.

From the main print, cut:

2 strips, 16½" x 42"; crosscut the strips into
    4 squares, 16½" x 16½"

4 strips, 6½" x 42"

From *each* of the 4 different fabrics of the same print, cut:

5 strips (20 total), 2½" x 42"

From the purple tone-on-tone print, cut:

6 strips, 3½" x 42"

From the medium blue tone-on-tone print, cut:

7 strips, 3½" x 42"

From the dark blue print, cut:

4 strips, 1½" x 42"

9 strips, 2¼" x 42"

From the multicolored print, cut:

9 strips, 6½" x 42"

Making the Blocks

1. Sew one 2½" x 42" strip of each of the four different print fabrics together to make a strip set as shown. Make five. Press the seams toward the darkest fabric. Crosscut the strip sets into 20 segments, 8½" wide. The segments should measure 8½" x 8½".

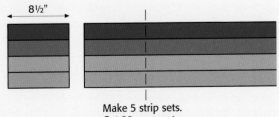

8½"

Make 5 strip sets.
Cut 20 segments.

2. Sew four segments together as shown to make a pieced block. Make five. The blocks should measure 16½" x 16½".

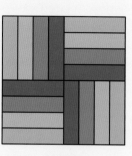

Make 5.

Assembling and Finishing the Quilt

1. Arrange the pieced blocks and main print 16½" squares into three rows as shown. Sew the blocks in each row together. Press the seams toward the plain blocks. Sew the rows together. Press the seams in one direction. The quilt top should now measure 48½" x 48½".

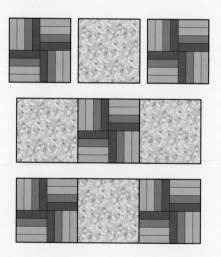

2. Refer to "Adding Borders" on page 12 to sew the 3½"-wide purple strips to your quilt top, followed

by the 3½"-wide medium blue strips. The quilt top should now measure 60½" x 60½".

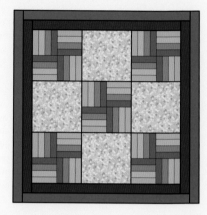

3. Refer to "Adding Borders" and the quilt diagram to sew the 6½"-wide main print strips to only the top and bottom edges of the quilt top, followed by the 1½"-wide dark blue strips, and then the 6½"-wide multicolored strips. Measure the quilt top for the side borders. Cut the remaining 6½"-wide multicolored strips to the length needed and sew them to the sides of the quilt top.

Quilt assembly

4. Refer to "Finishing Techniques" on page 13 for specific instructions on layering, quilting, and binding the quilt, and adding a label to the back. The quilt shown was quilted on a long-arm machine using the Flutterby pantograph designed by Linda Taylor of Linda's Electric Quilters (www.lequilters.com).

Quick-Strip Baby Quilt

Oh, baby! You won't find an easier quilt to make in this book. Perfect for a beginner, this project is just the thing when you need a *quick* baby or toddler gift.

Finished quilt size: 48" x 48"

Materials

Yardages are based on 42"-wide fabrics.

- ¼ yard *each* of 10 fabrics for quilt-top center (They can all be different or you can have some duplicates.)
- ¾ yard of juvenile print for outer border
- 3½ yards of fabric for backing
- ½ yard of fabric for binding
- 56" x 56" piece of batting

Cutting

All measurements include ¼"-wide seam allowances.

From *each* of the 10 fabrics for the center, cut:
1 strip (10 total), 4½" x 42"

From the juvenile print, cut:
5 strips, 4½" x 42"

From the binding fabric, cut:
6 strips, 2¼" x 42"

Assembling the Quilt

1. In the desired order, arrange the 10 strips for the quilt-top center as shown. Sew the strips together along the long edges. Press the seams open or in one direction. Square up the quilt top so that it measures 40½" x 40½".

2. Refer to "Adding Borders" on page 12 to sew the juvenile print 4½"-wide strips to the quilt top.

3. Refer to "Finishing Techniques" on page 13 for specific instructions on layering, quilting, and binding the quilt, and adding a label to the back.

Pastel prints in cozy flannel are the perfect pick for the newest member of the house.

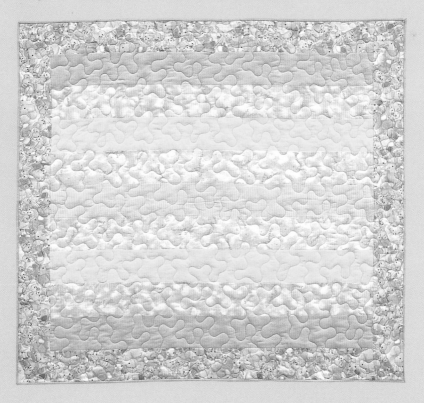

Spun Rail

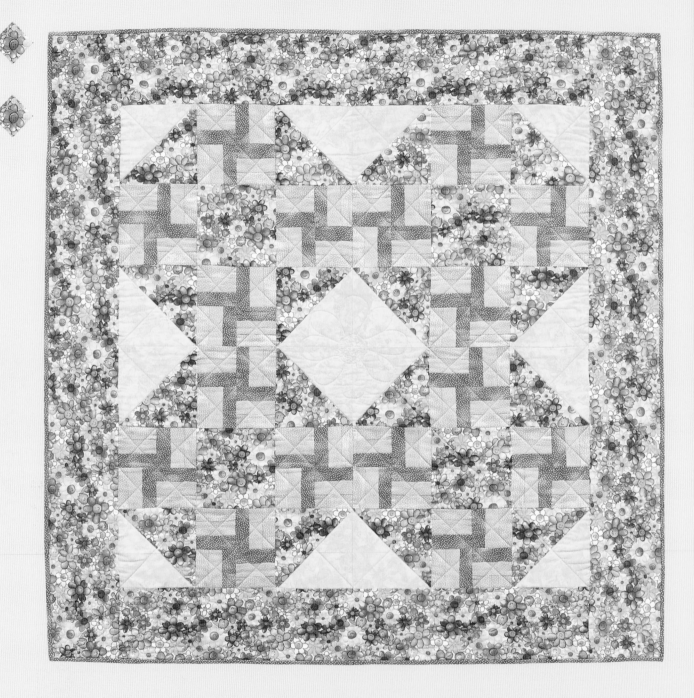

Combine rail fence units and half-square-triangle units to make the blocks for this *energetic* quilt. The more blocks you make, the bigger your quilt. Just *pick the size* you want from the four options included!

Baby-Size Spun Rail

Finished quilt size: 48" x 48"
Finished block size: 18" x 18"

Materials

Yardages are based on 42"-wide fabrics.

- 1¾ yards of multicolored print for block centers, half-square-triangle units, and border
- ½ yard of yellow fabric for block half-square-triangle units
- ⅜ yard *each* of dark, medium, and light prints for block rail fence units
- 3⅛ yards of fabric for backing
- ½ yard of fabric for binding
- 56" x 56" piece of batting

Cutting

All measurements include ¼"-wide seam allowances.

From the multicolored print, cut:

6 strips, 6½" x 42"; crosscut 1 strip into 4 squares, 6½" x 6½". Set aside the remaining strips for the border.

2 strips, 6⅞" x 42"; crosscut the strips into 8 squares, 6⅞" x 6⅞"

From the yellow fabric, cut:

2 strips, 6⅞" x 6⅞"; crosscut the strips into 8 squares, 6⅞" x 6⅞"

From *each* of the dark, medium, and light prints, cut:

6 strips (18 total), 1½" x 42"

From the binding fabric, cut:

6 strips, 2¼" x 42"

Making the Blocks

1. Place a 6⅞" multicolored square right sides together with a 6⅞" yellow square. Using a fabric marker or chalk, draw a diagonal line from corner to corner as shown. Sew ¼" from both sides of the diagonal line.

2. Cut on the marked line to create two units. Press the seams open and trim off the "mouse ears." Each half-square-triangle unit should measure 6½" x 6½".

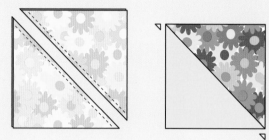

3. Repeat steps 1 and 2 with the remaining 6⅞" squares to make 16 half-square-triangle units. Set the units aside.

4. Sew one 1½" x 42" strip of each of the three different prints together along the long edges to make a strip set. Make six. Press the seams open. Crosscut the strip sets into 64 segments, 3½" wide.

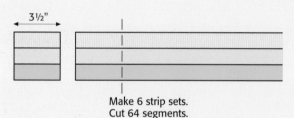

**Make 6 strip sets.
Cut 64 segments.**

5. Sew four segments from step 4 together as shown. Make 16. Press the seams open. Each rail fence unit should measure 6½" x 6½".

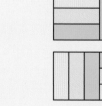
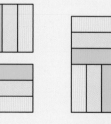

Make 16.

6. Arrange four half-square-triangle units, four rail fence units, and one 6½" multicolored square into three horizontal rows as shown. Sew the units in each row together. Press the seams in

opposite directions from row to row. Sew the rows together to complete the block. Press the seams in one direction. Make four. The blocks should measure 18½" x 18½".

Make 4.

Assembling and Finishing the Quilt

1. Arrange the blocks in horizontal rows as shown. Sew the blocks in each row together. Press the seams in opposite directions from row to row. Sew the rows together. Press the seams in one direction.

2. Refer to "Adding Borders" on page 12 to sew the 6½"-wide multicolored strips to the quilt top.

3. Refer to "Finishing Techniques" on page 13 for specific instructions on layering, quilting, and binding the quilt, and adding a label to the back.

Quilt assembly

Twin-Size Spun Rail

Finished quilt size: 66" x 84"
Finished block size: 18" x 18"

Materials

Yardages are based on 42"-wide fabrics.

- 3⅛ yards of multicolored print for block centers, half-square-triangle units, and border
- 1⅛ yards of yellow fabric for block half-square-triangle units
- 1 yard *each* of dark, medium, and light prints for block rail fence units
- 5⅛ yards of fabric for backing
- ¾ yard of fabric for binding
- 74" x 92" piece of batting

Cutting

All measurements include ¼"-wide seam allowances.

From the multicolored print, cut:

10 strips, 6½" x 42"; crosscut 2 strips into
   12 squares, 6½" x 6½". Set aside the remaining strips for the border.

5 strips, 6⅞" x 42"; crosscut the strips into
   24 squares, 6⅞" x 6⅞".

From the yellow fabric, cut:

5 strips, 6⅞" x 42"; crosscut the strips into
   24 squares, 6⅞" x 6⅞".

From *each* of the dark, medium, and light prints, cut:

18 strips (54 total), 1½" x 42"

From the binding fabric, cut:

9 strips, 2¼" x 42"

Assembling the Quilt

Refer to the steps indicated for "Baby-Size Spun Rail" on page 51 to complete the blocks and finish the quilt.

1. Refer to steps 1 and 2 to make 48 half-square-triangle units.

2. Refer to step 4 to make 18 strip sets and crosscut them into 192 segments.

3. Refer to step 5 to make 48 rail fence units.

4. Follow step 6 to make 12 blocks.

5. Assemble and finish the quilt as instructed in "Assembling and Finishing the Quilt."

Quilt assembly

Queen-Size Spun Rail

Finished quilt size: 84" x 102"
Finished block size: 18" x 18"

Materials

Yardages are based on 42"-wide fabrics.

- 4½ yards of multicolored print for block centers, half-square-triangle units, and border
- 1¾ yards of yellow fabric for block half-square-triangle units
- 1¾ yards *each* of dark, medium, and light prints for block rail fence units
- 8 yards of fabric for backing
- ⅞ yard of fabric for binding
- 92" x 110" piece of batting

Cutting

All measurements include ¼"-wide seam allowances.

From the multicolored print, cut:

14 strips, 6½" x 42"; crosscut 4 strips into
    20 squares, 6½" x 6½". Set aside the remaining strips for the border.
8 strips, 6⅞" x 42"; crosscut the strips into
    40 squares, 6⅞" x 6⅞"

From the yellow fabric, cut:

8 strips, 6⅞" x 42"; crosscut the strips into
    40 squares, 6⅞" x 6⅞"

From *each* of the light, medium, and dark prints, cut:

30 strips (90 total), 1½" x 42"

From the binding fabric, cut:

11 strips, 2¼" x 42"

Assembling the Quilt

Refer to the steps indicated for "Baby-Size Spun Rail" on page 51 to complete the blocks and finish the quilt.

1. Refer to steps 1 and 2 to make 80 half-square-triangle units.

2. Refer to step 4 to make 30 strip sets and crosscut them into 320 segments.

3. Refer to step 5 to make 80 rail fence units.

4. Follow step 6 to make 20 blocks.

5. Assemble and finish the quilt as instructed in "Assembling and Finishing the Quilt."

Quilt assembly

King-Size Spun Rail

Finished quilt size: 120" x 120"
Finished block size: 18" x 18"

Materials

Yardages are based on 42"-wide fabrics.

- 6⅞ yards of multicolored print for block centers, half-square-triangle units, and border
- 3¼ yards of yellow fabric for block half-square-triangle units
- 2½ yards *each* of dark, medium, and light prints for block rail fence units
- 14¼ yards of fabric for backing
- 1⅛ yards of fabric for binding
- 128" x 128" piece of batting

Cutting

All measurements include ¼"-wide seam allowances.

From the multicolored print, cut:

18 strips, 6½" x 42"; crosscut 6 strips into
    36 squares, 6½" x 6½". Set aside the remaining strips for the border.

15 strips, 6⅞" x 42"; crosscut the strips into
    72 squares, 6⅞" x 6⅞"

From the black print, cut:

15 strips, 6⅞" x 42"; crosscut the strips into
    72 squares, 6⅞" x 6⅞"

From *each* of the dark, medium, and light prints, cut:

53 strips (159 total), 1½" x 42"

From the binding fabric, cut:

14 strips, 2¼" x 42"

Assembling the Quilt

Refer to the steps indicated for "Baby-Size Spun Rail" on page 51 to complete the blocks and finish the quilt.

1. Refer to steps 1 and 2 to make 144 half-square-triangle units.

2. Refer to step 4 to make 53 strip sets and crosscut them into 576 segments.

3. Refer to step 5 to make 144 rail fence units.

4. Follow step 6 to make 30 blocks.

5. Assemble and finish the quilt as instructed in "Assembling and Finishing the Quilt."

Quilt assembly

In this twin-size version of the Spun Rail quilt, a black background sets off the bold colors of the rail fence units.

Twisted Strips

Gather five fat quarters for the blocks and a coordinating fabric for the setting triangles and border, and you're ready to make this octagonal table topper. Be sure to select a batting that will allow the topper to *drape* nicely over the table edges.

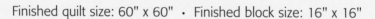

Finished quilt size: 60" x 60" · Finished block size: 16" x 16"

Materials

Yardages are based on 42"-wide fabrics.

- 2¼ yards of cream print for setting triangles and border
- 1 fat quarter *each* of 5 different fabrics for blocks
- 3⅞ yards of fabric for backing
- ⅝ yard of fabric for binding
- 68" x 68" piece of batting

FAT-QUARTER FACTS

- Fat quarters can vary in size, depending on the original width of the fabric. You will need fat quarters that measure at least 18" x 21".
- When you cut the strips, place the longest edge closest to your body and cut along the shorter edge as shown.

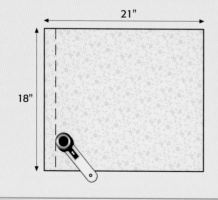

Cutting

All measurements include ¼"-wide seam allowances. Before you begin cutting, label five sandwich-size plastic storage bags with the following piece numbers: 1, 2, 3/4, 5/6, and 7. As you cut the numbered pieces, place them in the corresponding bags. This will make later steps much easier to do.

From *each* of the 5 different fat quarters, cut:

1 strip (5 total), 5" x 18". From each strip, cut:
    1 square (5 total), 4½" x 4½" (piece 1)
    2 rectangles (10 total), 2½" x 12½" (piece 5)
6 strips (30 total), 2½" x 18". Crosscut the strips into:
    2 rectangles (10 total), 2½" x 16½" (piece 7)
    2 rectangles (10 total), 2½" x 12½" (piece 6)
    4 rectangles (20 total), 2½" x 8½"
      (pieces 3 and 4)
    2 rectangles (10 total), 2½" x 4½" (piece 2)

From the cream print, cut:

1 square, 23⅞" x 23⅞"; cut the square in half twice diagonally to yield 4 triangles
7 strips, 6½" x 42"

From the binding fabric, cut:

7 strips, 2¼" x 42"

Making the Blocks

1. Randomly select one piece 1 and two *each* of pieces 2–7 from the corresponding bags.

2. Arrange the pieces as shown.

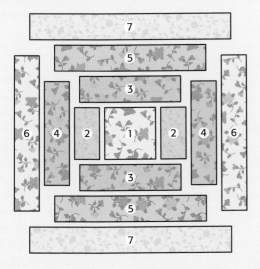

3. Repeat steps 1 and 2 to arrange a total of five blocks. Rearrange the pieces between blocks as necessary until you're satisfied with the layout of each block.

4. For each block, sew the pieces together in numerical order. The blocks should measure 16½" x 16½".

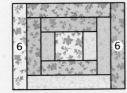

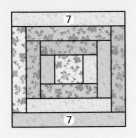

Make 5.

Assembling and Finishing the Table Topper

1. Arrange the blocks and the cream triangles into three rows as shown. Sew the pieces in each row together. Press the seams in the directions indicated. Sew the rows together. Press the seams in one direction.

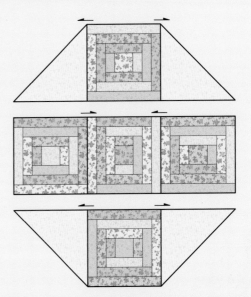

2. Center and sew the cream 6½"-wide strips to the short sides of the table topper. Trim the strips even with the long sides as shown.

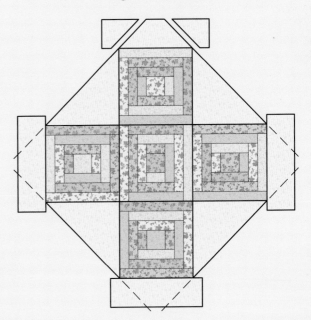

3. Refer to "Adding Borders" on page 12 to measure the table topper through the center. Piece and cut four cream strips to the length measured. Sew the strips to the long sides of the table topper. Trim the ends even with the short sides as shown.

4. Refer to "Finishing Techniques" on page 13 for specific instructions on layering, quilting, and binding the quilt, and adding a label to the back. The quilt shown was quilted on a long-arm machine using the Springtime Flower Meandering pantograph designed by Sophie Collier of Sew-Phie Quilts (763-323-7736).

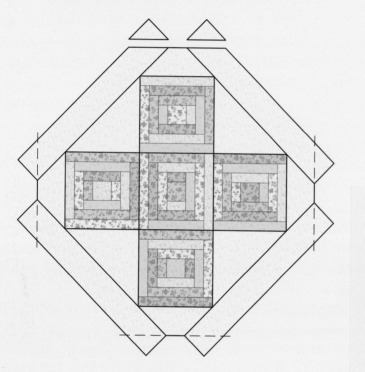

Make this table topper into a tree skirt by cutting a slit up the side and a hole in the center. Be sure to use bias binding around the center hole.

Pillowcase

Make a *fast* and *simple* standard-size pillowcase to coordinate with a quilt or to give as a *gift!*

Finished pillowcase size: 19½" x 29"

Materials

Yardages are based on 42"-wide fabrics.

- ¾ yard of main fabric for body
- ⅜ yard of coordinating fabric for cuff
- ⅛ yard of coordinating fabric for accent

Cutting

All measurements include ¼"-wide seam allowances.
Cut off the selvage edges of fabric before beginning.

From the accent fabric, cut:

1 strip, 2½" x 40"

From the main fabric for the body, cut:

1 rectangle, 24" x 40"

From the cuff fabric, cut:

1 strip, 12" x 40"

Assembling the Pillowcase

1. Press the accent strip in half lengthwise, wrong sides together. Repeat with the cuff strip.

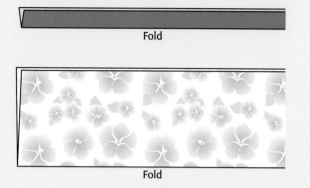

2. With the raw edges aligned, pin the folded accent strip to the right side of the pillowcase body rectangle along one long edge. Don't stitch yet.

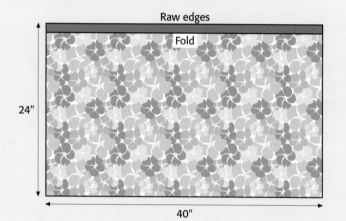

3. Pin the folded cuff strip over the accent strip, aligning the raw edges. Sew ¼" from the long raw edges through all of the layers. Zigzag stitch along the edges to prevent raveling.

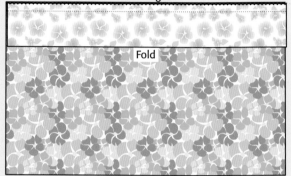

4. Press the seam toward the pillowcase body. Turn the piece to the right side and press the accent strip toward the cuff. Then trim any uneven edges along the short sides.

5. Fold the piece in half along the 40" edge, right sides together. Sew ¼" from the side and bottom edges as shown. Clean-finish the edges with a zigzag stitch or serge the edges.

6. Turn the pillowcase to the right side; press.

About the Author

Ann Kisro lives in Rochester, Minnesota, and works at her parents' quilt shop, the Quilting Cupboard. Shortly after the shop opened in July 2003, Ann started quilting and designing her first patterns. A year later, at age 19, she wrote her very first quilting book for Martingale & Company. She counts being Martingale's youngest author as one of her greatest accomplishments. Ann has an associate's degree in retail merchandising and interior decorating and loves designing, working with fabric, traveling, and being outdoors. Come and visit Ann at the Quilting Cupboard in Rochester, or visit the shop's Web site at www.thequiltingcupboard.com.

New and Bestselling Titles from

Martingale® & COMPANY

America's Best-Loved Craft & Hobby Books®
America's Best-Loved Knitting Books®

That Patchwork Place®

America's Best-Loved Quilt Books®

NEW RELEASES
Alphabet Soup
Big Knitting
Big 'n Easy
Courtship Quilts
Crazy Eights
Creating Your Perfect Quilting Space
Crochet from the Heart
Fabulous Flowers
First Crochet
Fun and Funky Crochet
Joined at the Heart
Little Box of Knitted Ponchos and Wraps, The
Little Box of Knitted Throws, The
Merry Christmas Quilts
More Crocheted Aran Sweaters
Party Time!
Perfectly Brilliant Knits
Polka-Dot Kids' Quilts
Quilt Block Bonanza
Quilts from Grandmother's Garden
Raise the Roof
Saturday Sweaters
Save the Scraps
Seeing Stars
Sensational Knitted Socks
Sensational Sashiko
Strip-Pieced Quilts
Tea in the Garden
Treasury of Scrap Quilts, A

Our books are available at bookstores and your favorite craft, fabric, and yarn retailers.
If you don't see the title you're looking for, visit us at
www.martingale-pub.com
or contact us at:
1-800-426-3126

International: 1-425-483-3313
Fax: 1-425-486-7596
Email: info@martingale-pub.com

06/05

APPLIQUÉ
Appliqué Takes Wing
Easy Appliqué Samplers
Garden Party
Stitch and Split Appliqué
Sunbonnet Sue: All through the Year
WOW! Wool-on-Wool Folk-Art Quilts

LEARNING TO QUILT
101 Fabulous Rotary-Cut Quilts
Happy Endings, Revised Edition
Loving Stitches, Revised Edition
Magic of Quiltmaking, The
Quilter's Quick Reference Guide, The
Sensational Settings, Revised Edition
Your First Quilt Book (or it should be!)

PAPER PIECING
40 Bright and Bold Paper-Pieced Blocks
50 Fabulous Paper-Pieced Stars
300 Paper-Pieced Quilt Blocks
Easy Machine Paper Piecing
Fanciful Quilts to Paper Piece
Hooked on Triangles
Quilter's Ark, A
Show Me How to Paper Piece

QUILTS FOR BABIES & CHILDREN
American Doll Quilts
Even More Quilts for Baby
More Quilts for Baby
Quilts for Baby
Sweet and Simple Baby Quilts

ROTARY CUTTING/SPEED PIECING
40 Fabulous Quick-Cut Quilts
365 Quilt Blocks a Year: Perpetual Calendar
1000 Great Quilt Blocks
Clever Quilts Encore
Endless Stars
Once More around the Block
Square Dance, Revised Edition
Stack a New Deck
Star-Studded Quilts
Strips and Strings

SCRAP QUILTS
More Nickel Quilts
Nickel Quilts
Scrap Frenzy
Successful Scrap Quilts

TOPICS IN QUILTMAKING
Basket Bonanza
Cottage-Style Quilts
Everyday Folk Art
Focus on Florals
Follow the Dots . . . to Dazzling Quilts
Log Cabin Quilts
More Biblical Quilt Blocks
Quilter's Home: Spring, The
Scatter Garden Quilts
Shortcut to Drunkard's Path, A
Strawberry Fair
Summertime Quilts
Tried and True
Warm Up to Wool

CRAFTS
Bag Boutique
Collage Cards
Creating with Paint
Painted Fabric Fun
Purely Primitive
Stamp in Color
Trashformations
Vintage Workshop, The: Gifts for All Occasions
Year of Cats...in Hats!, A

KNITTING & CROCHET
200 Knitted Blocks
365 Knitting Stitches a Year: Perpetual Calendar
Classic Crocheted Vests
Crocheted Socks!
Dazzling Knits
First Knits
Handknit Style
Knitted Throws and More for the Simply Beautiful Home
Knitting with Hand-Dyed Yarns
Little Box of Crocheted Hats and Scarves, The
Little Box of Scarves, The
Little Box of Scarves II, The
Little Box of Sweaters, The
Pleasures of Knitting, The
Pursenalities
Rainbow Knits for Kids
Sarah Dallas Knitting
Ultimate Knitted Tee, The